GETTING STARTED AS A
MEDIATOR

Seven Steps to Starting and Building a Successful Mediation Practice

Clay Phillips

WHY THE CHESSBOARD COVER?

Chess is well-known as the ultimate game of strategy. The strategy of chess is based entirely in the players' ability to *think ahead* through several different scenarios - scenarios of how they and their opponent will respond to each other's moves as the game progresses. Thus, while very nerve wracking, chess isn't a game that can be mastered by or through emotion-driven decision making. The chess master *chooses* to not allow emotions to govern his decisions, rather the consequences of the decisions he has not yet made. The *human conflict condition* is very similar to chess in that, regardless the amount of thought we put into our decisions, there will be an outcome, and a consequence for every decision we make. What makes humans uniquely different from each other isn't the decisions we make, but *why we choose* to make emotion-driven decisions. In this context, we each play multiple games of *intrapersonal, interpersonal and extra-personal chess* simultaneously every day.

MIDDLE MAN
PRESS
NASHVILLE • TENNESSEE

ISBN-13: 978-0-9992723-0-5

Mediation has been in the top 50 new and emerging careers in the US since 2012. Now non-attorney mediators are more popular than ever but there's just one problem... No one is teaching new mediators *(attorney mediators and non-attorney mediators alike)* how to enter the profession with any margin of success. That is, until now... until I wrote this book.

DEDICATION

This book is dedicated to all the mediators and graduate/doctoral students I have trained and taught over the last decade. I thank you each for trusting me to inform and educate you about the mediation craft, and allowing me to be a part of this journey in your life.

CONTENTS

1. GETTING INFORMED

Like any other important venture in your life, you need to be reliably informed about mediation as well as how the state or states in which you plan to operate *define* the practice of mediation in court and other professional settings. So, first let's start with the assumption that your state(s) has a regulatory agency for oversight of the practice of mediation. In most states, that agency is a subordinate body *(commission or committee)* of the state's Supreme Court. In some states, the regulatory agency might be within the Department of Human Services. Usually, the best place to start to identify this agency is a simple Internet search of "//your state// requirements for mediators".

As of this writing, 28 of the 50 US states have comprehensive standards to be recognized as a mediator in their courts. Of these 28 states, 25 have higher standards for those wishing to mediate domestic disputes *(divorce, parentage, Child Support)* than civil disputes *(non-domestic, non-criminal)*. Of the remaining 22 states, nine (9) have some requirements for those wishing to mediate domestic disputes.

Regardless the state, these standards and requirements typically consist of three key elements: education, relevant work experience, and mediation training. Four (4) states require a law degree to qualify as a civil mediator, while five (5) require specific education *(bachelor's or graduate degree)* in relevant fields, and specific work/professional experience. In some situations, a well-founded waiver request may allow the individual to forego certain requirements. The training requirement for mediators will also vary by state. Most of the 28 states require successful completion of pre-approved training programs in civil and domestic mediation, and mediation involving domestic violence issues. These training requirements are all state-specific. It is important to know that each of these requirements must be met to be approved as a court mediator.

So, first you will need to determine which types of court cases you plan to mediate and then determine what the requirements are for that certification. Generally, most states place a more rigid approval criteria for domestic *(Family Law and Juvenile Law)* mediators than civil mediators this is because Family Law and Juvenile Law are more highly specialized than other lawsuits *(contractual effect of a marriage and marital property, and providing for the health and care of a minor child or children within and without a marriage).* Family Law mediation deals with matters between married and previously married parties *(division of marital assets and debt, co-parenting plans, Child Support)*, while Juvenile Law mediation deals with providing for and protecting minor children, most of whom are born outside of wedlock of the parents *(co-parenting plans, Child Support,)*. The General Civil mediator mediates all other civil lawsuits such as personal injury, products liability, landlord-tenant, contracts, Real Estate transactions, construction, wrongful death, professional malpractice, conservatorships, Will and estate contests, etc.

Of the hundreds of mediators I've trained over the last decade, I estimate that roughly one-third plan/planned to obtain both Family/Juvenile and General Civil Mediator certificates. Their rationale vary some, but most tell me that they want to get exposed to as many different types of cases *(as a mediator)* so they can better determine which area of practice is the best fit for them. Others tell me that they become dual-certified because they want all the training and experience they can get. I believe each of these are very valid reasons for becoming a mediator because it's a very personal journey that the mediator must experience by themselves and for themselves.

Once you have identified your niche *(market segment)* as a Family/Juvenile or General Civil mediator - or both, it's time to find out the specific qualification requirements to mediate those cases in your state(s). Here is an overview of what the requirements you can expect:

Education requirement. As an *unofficial* rule, the several states that require regulatory pre-approval to become a court mediator place a great emphasis on the education requirement. These basic educational requirements will be very similar to this:

- Family / Juvenile Law Mediator: a minimum of a graduate degree (Master's, JD, or higher) is required;
- General Civil: a minimum of a bachelor's or baccalaureate degree is required.

Relevant professional experience requirement. The key here is that most states use the language *relevant* work or professional experience when referring to this requirement. The reason I highlight this is because *most* of the people my staff and I consult with *(pre-training)* are under the impression that you have to be an attorney to be a court mediator when that isn't true in most states. Granted, some states do require court mediators to be licensed attorneys, but the majority do not. So, *relevant work / professional experience* is typically interpreted as experience that demonstrates your professional ability and expertise to assist others in resolving their problems. That said, this is inclusive of many different professions and callings like: customer service, supervision and management, business owners, Human

Resource professionals, Mental Health professionals, educators, clergy, etc.. So, don't be too quick to exclude yourself just because you aren't an attorney or you don't have a legal background. Think about your professional background - about each job you've had - and ask yourself this simple question: *"Did my job rely on my helping others solve problems related to their lives or work, or both?"* If the answer is *yes*, I'd bet you meet this requirement. Last, most states will define the minimum number of years of relevant work/professional experience required to be a court mediator. That's simple, just add the years of your experience *(across all jobs)* and you'll have your number.

Mediator training requirement. Next, you'll need to get informed about the requirements for being a mediator in each state that you plan to serve. So be sure to locate and make contact with the current program manager to ensure you understand these standards and requirements. As time goes by, more and more states seem to be aligning their training requirements with each other and are creating somewhat of a standard, with some states being more detailed and rigorous than others. For example, Florida has the most detailed qualification system in place compared to the other states. Most states (Florida included) require between 30 and 40 hours of approved basic mediator training for both Family/Juvenile Law mediators and General Civil mediators, as well as an additional six (6) hours of Family/Juvenile Law specific to each state. Generally, these six additional hours of Family/Juvenile Law focus on the Rights of the parents, the Rights of all subject minor children, provisions for the care, nurturing and financial support of all subject minor children.

Last, once you have decided which types of cases you plan to mediate and have adequately educated yourself on the exact training requirements you will need to meet, it's time to locate and call the approved trainers in your area and find out when and where they will offer the training you need. When you contact these trainers, I urge you to prepare a list of questions having to do with the mediator certification process to help you decide which trainer's program you want to attend. It's critical that you find the best training possible so you get off on the right foot - not to mention it is a substantial financial investment. You will find these approved trainers through your state's regulatory agency *(usually on their website)*, and will find them included with Appendix A. If you have located or contacted a trainer that does not appear on this agency's list of approved trainers, you will need to find one that does. Additionally, I believe it is fair for you to ask each trainer how long they have been an approved mediator trainer, how many mediators they have trained, if they have an active mediation practice, and how many and what types of cases they've mediated. Also, be sure to ask if they have any reviews published by their trainees so you can see what others are saying about them and their training. The cost of training will vary from state to state and from trainer to trainer, so be sure to compare the cost… but remember, cheaper isn't necessarily better. So, consider your time and financial investment and get the most and best experience you can.

2. GETTING TRAINED & CERTIFIED

Once you've made contact with the state regulatory agency for mediation, you should also ask the program manager for referrals to approved mediator training programs *(if training is required by the state)*. While some states (i.e. Arizona, Texas, etc.) do not have formal mediator training requirements or regulation, please do not see this as a carte blanche opportunity to seize a mediation career. Regulation of every professional practice is best when balanced - enough regulation, but not too much. No regulation at all isn't enough and can present a myriad of opportunities to exposure and liability that you probably cannot sustain.

Be sure to contact the approved trainers in your area to gauge their program structure and training style. Ask them what kind of training environment and experience can you expect. Determine the best fit for your needs and register for the training as soon as you can and are ready. Remember that this will likely be a very substantial investment of your time, money, and lost wages during the training period, so choose your trainer carefully. Ask each trainer if they will provide any assistance or support to you after you complete training. I believe this is a very reasonable question, if not expectation. As a mediator trainer, I am honored that so many people trust me with a part of their professional and career development and I think it is only fair that I offer to support them any way I can after they have completed their mediator training with me.

After you have completed the required mediator training program(s), your state(s) may require you to conduct several mediations before you are fully eligible to apply for mediator certification/approval. Generally, if you do not have ready access to a mediation mentor, you will be able to observe and conduct supervised mediation on your local courts' *pro se* dockets *(not represented by an attorney)*. To locate these dockets, simply call your local Court Clerk(s) for times, dates, locations, and judges' names. Most judges have at least one pro se docket and are extremely open and amenable to using mediation to help move the docket along. Do not assume that just because a case is pro se the parties are unable to pay mediator fees. This is a common misconception and should be addressed on a case-by-case basis. In any case, if a party is unable to afford to pay the mediator, that party should ask the court to declare them indigent - for these purposes.

Be smart, be accessible, be responsive, and be available. By being smart, you are constantly aware of your surroundings - both collegial and consumer surroundings. Engage people where they are and when you meet with them. By being accessible you are telling your colleagues and constituents that you care and that you are aware that you may be the ideal mediator for any given case, situation, or parties... heck, you might be their only chance at settling a case. Be sensitive and responsive to the financial needs of the parties whose case you will mediate. Not everyone can afford the fees of a mediator, so be sure to respond when those who are unable to pay you need your skills. By being available you are demonstrating that you are grounded and your overriding purpose is to help others. Be smart, accessible, responsive, and available... it's how you demonstrate your character.

Remember, your mediator training is only going to take you so far, so be sure to have a strategic plan for the following days, weeks, and months. Have a plan to accomplish the following, every step of the way:

- Get experience mediating. One of the best ways to test and hone your new mediation skills is to spend as much time volunteering your mediation services as possible. This is also one of the best ways to meet judges and attorneys, as well as build your mediator network. Most Juvenile Courts across the country are begging for mediators to volunteer their time settling co-parenting disputes that continue to appear on their dockets.

- Keep a mediator's journal. Your career as a mediator will be a process of learning and growing, so record everything important you learn. Write down the dates and places you meet people like judges, attorneys, court clerks, other related staff, and business professionals. You will find quickly that the mediation field and legal profession are very small, big worlds. It's not that everyone knows everyone, but almost everyone knows almost everyone... so make and keep a plan to make that happen. Your journal will help you do that and make sense of a very busy career.

- Stay informed and inform others. While the mediation field and legal profession are fairly static when it comes to changes in law and procedure, changes do occur routinely. What this means is that a law doesn't necessarily have to change completely or in a complex way for a change to be significant. Just think if the word "only" is removed from a law, or the word "should" is changed to "shall" - or vice versa. Laws and court rules are subject to scrutiny and change every day and it will be your responsibility to be aware of and understand these changes. One of the best ways I discovered to stay apprised of these changes is to teach others about these changes - changes that are relevant to my expertise. For example, if a law changes regarding mediation in Tennessee Courts I immediately contact the Tennessee Supreme Court Administrative Office of the Courts and ask for every definition and opinion they have on this new law. I also ask attorneys, judges, and other mediators what their view of the changes are. Then I combine all of this input, create a workshop and offer it to the same groups of professionals as a discussion leader. Gaining an audience is as easy as going to the county Bar Associations and offering to provide a free Continuing Legal Education (CLE) course during their monthly meetings.

3. GETTING CONNECTED

After you have identified the courts and dockets that you plan to serve, and/or have begun to mediate as a volunteer on pro se or other dockets, build this time into your schedule. To get started as a mediator, you have to reserve and invest time: time to continually hone your mediation skills and time to build your network.

In addition to your mediation skills and acumen (voluntary or for hire), your success as a mediator is going to depend on the relationships you build with other professionals. Meeting judges, attorneys, and court staff is one thing… connecting with them is another.

A key strategic element of creating and building a network in the legal field is to first understand and accept a few components on which you can rely with great predictability:

- Lawyers and judges are sworn to an extremely high level of ethical conduct that encompasses their entire lives. They can't turn it on and off. Know that while a great sense of humor can contribute to great success and a long career, if you are a light-hearted person or even a bit of a jokester, don't take their dry response as an indication that they have no interest in your or your offerings. Just make sure that your tone and rhetoric match the seriousness of the topic at hand.

- Lawyers and judges are typically very busy. Even if you see them in what appears to be a relaxed and disengaged setting, it is probably a momentary break in a very full and often complicated daily schedule. Why am I telling you this? Because they won't have time to talk with you about a concept or an idea you have. Rather, think your concept/idea through to fruition, consider best and worst case scenarios, reconsider the validity and veracity of your concept/idea, establish the concept as a real working model by using my ADTIME™ method: *Assess - Design - Test - Implement - Monitor - Evaluate*. If you can move your concept/idea successfully through this method, you more likely have something they will want to know about.

- Lawyers and judges can be fickle - and rightfully so - about *outsiders* within the legal profession. Outsiders meaning non-attorneys, non-paralegals, non-clerks, non-law enforcement. Just remember that if you fall into one or more of these categories, you will need to earn their collegial respect before you are trusted enough to fully enter the fold. Be patient and keep in mind everything I've told you so far. In other words, the legal profession is not a machine or anything that resembles a mechanism of any kind. It is an extremely dynamic and multi-dimensional environment filled with highly passionate, highly skilled, and educated people who are there because they love what they do and why they do it. It might even be a little difficult to get to their level of excitement and entrenchment, but your best opportunity is to show genuine interest in what they do and respect how very little *spare time* they have. Point being, be prepared when you meet or speak with them… always. If your idea is something they can benefit from, start by asking them if they have the problem that your idea will fix. If they answer *yes*, ask them how often they have the problem. Then ask them if they would be interested in hearing a "solution that you have created" to address that problem. When they say *yes*, you're on. Keep it under five (5) minutes. You've already discussed the problem enough, and they know the pain it creates. Get to the solution first. "So, this is what my solution does…//describe it - don't explain it//" and "this is how it works". Then stop talking/selling and let them think and ask you questions. Quiet mouse. Don't talk. Wait. Wait until they talk. Remember, in negotiations, *he who speaks first loses*.

In the majority of states, mediation is considered a function of the judiciary. Meaning that the mediator ultimately works for and reports to the judge where the case is filed. The parties pay your fees, but you work for the judge. In some cases (generally involving parenting issues) the state might subsidize your pay if one or both of the parties are indigent. The same program manager at your state regulatory agency should be able to answer that question for you and provide you with all the information you need in that regard.

In the mediation setting, only the attorneys have *clients*. We mediators do not. That said, mediators must always be mindful of and practice the highest level of judicial ethics and objectivity. What does this mean? It means that you - the mediator - are representing the judicial process, and the judge and you must do everything within your power to insure that this case is in better shape than when you got involved. By *better shape* I mean that, after mediation, the parties should have a much better idea of what some likely and uncertain circumstances and outcomes might be if they do not settle at mediation and end up at trial. The mediator's position is one of integrity, trust, and public confidence and every mediator should execute it accordingly. Judicial behavior of the mediator is one that reflects the highest level of objectivity, mutual respect, impartiality, fairness, procedural flexibility, self-determination, third party empowerment, and steadfast abstinence from judgment and counsel. The mediator's judicial behavior also extends to the relationships they have with the judiciary and their staff. While building your network of judges, be careful not to inadvertently violate that trust by giving or offering inducements of any kind *(to the judge or anyone on their staff)* to secure employment with them. In other words, do not give judges or their staff gifts in any form – as an example. Finally, the judicial behavior of the mediator must always honor their pledge of confidentiality and privacy to the parties and the process. This includes prohibition of conversations about any mediation with anyone other than the parties and their attorneys. For clarity, *anyone* includes judges.

Last, but certainly not least, to ensure your best start and launch as a private practice mediator, you must be a *joiner*. A joiner is a professional that actively seeks out every association, organization, cause or entity that promotes his or her profession in any way. Some examples for mediators to join include Bar associations, SHRM (Society for Human Resource Management), Chambers of Commerce, community mediation centers, Rotary, etc. If you aren't a joiner, become one. Choose the professional associations you join carefully and make sure they can and will provide an immediate return on your investment (your time and money).

I recommend joining every Bar Association in your area (that allows for non-attorney members, for non-attorney mediators). Many Bar Associations will allow non-attorney members as associate members. Attend as many Bar

Association mixers and functions you can – and take plenty of business cards along with a practiced shtick about who you are and what you have to offer.

SHRM is an incredible organization that is comprised of Human Resource professionals throughout the local area (they're a lot more qualified to be your customer than members of a Chamber, but don't forsake Chambers… I'll tell you why in a moment). Think about it, HR professionals are mediation machines, even though they probably have never been trained as a mediator. Our HR comrades spend their entire day, week, month, quarter, and year helping others with their problems… they know what mediation is, they understand it, they love it and they want to know mediators. Many HR professionals have hired me to mediate internal and external disputes as well as to provide onsite training to their staff and other employees. So you see, your relationship with HR professionals could and should be multi-faceted and multi-dimensional based on their needs.

Next, Chambers of Commerce and Rotary. Please don't make the mistake many *self-employeds* and entrepreneurs make and convince yourself that you don't need to join and participate in your local Chamber(s) or Rotary. Businesses of all sizes and every size join and stay actively involved in Chambers and Rotary, and so should you. Besides, why wouldn't you want to be in a room full of decision-makers that need help with the conflict in their business lives? Join today and participate.

Community mediation centers can be found with a simple Internet search. Find the ones nearest you, make contact, ask them how you can help and go help them. Part of your obligation to the mediation profession is to make yourself available to assist your fellow citizens that may not have the financial wherewithal to afford to pay a professional mediator like you. It is incumbent upon all mediators to make sure that no one misses out on professional mediation services simply because they don't have the ability to pay for it.

4. STEP ONE: LOCATE YOURSELF

Where are you right now? Physically? Geographically? Are you where you need to be? Are you where you want to be? If you could wave a magic wand and be where you want to be (physically/geographically) where would that be? If you're not there right now, is it a deal-breaker for being a mediator? If it is, what is the probability that that will/can change soon enough to pursue your mediation career? If you're not there and you can be there, craft a plan and align it with your other plans to start and build your mediation practice. What is your current *career transition condition*?

Where are you in life? Age? Health? Personal happiness? Personal commitments? Professional happiness? Professional commitments? Financial security? How are these connected individually? How are these connected collectively? Does one or more rely more heavily on another? If so, which ones are they?

Create a diagram of each of these, and assign a score from 0 to 10 (zero being the lowest and ten being the highest) as to how favorable each is to you while establishing yourself as a mediator and starting a mediation career. Think of it like this, ask yourself these questions:

1. Is my age a hindrance or an advantage in this endeavor? *Yes* would be closer to zero than ten, and *No* would be closer to 10 than zero.

2. Is my health a hindrance or an advantage in this endeavor? *Yes* would be closer to zero than ten, and *No* would be closer to 10 than zero.

3. Is my personal happiness a hindrance or an advantage in this endeavor? *Yes* would be closer to zero than ten, and *No* would be closer to 10 than zero.

4. Are my personal commitments a hindrance or an advantage in this endeavor? *Yes* would be closer to zero than ten, and *No* would be closer to 10 than zero.

5. Is my professional happiness a hindrance or an advantage in this endeavor? *Yes* would be closer to zero than ten, and *No* would be closer to 10 than zero.

6. Are my professional commitments a hindrance or an advantage in this endeavor? *Yes* would be closer to zero than ten, and *No* would be closer to 10 than zero.

7. Is my financial security a hindrance or an advantage in this endeavor? *Yes* would be closer to zero than ten, and *No* would be closer to 10 than zero.

Write your scores here *(be honest and judicious with your scoring)*:

_____ Age

_____ Health

_____ Personal Happiness

_____ Personal Commitments   **My Total Score:** _____

_____ Professional Happiness

_____ Professional Commitments

_____ Financial Security

Now, total your scores. The **lowest** *healthy score* is **36** and the **highest** healthy score is **70**. So, if you scored **below 36**, you will likely want to evaluate your answers/assessment to make sure your individual scores are accurate and your math is correct. If your total score is indeed below 36, it probably isn't the best time for you to make this career change. Surprisingly perhaps, the healthiest total score will not be 70, rather within the 70-90% range or between 49 and 63. This is because a score of 70 indicates that your are in the absolute best place and time in your life to pursue this career transition. It isn't that 70 is an impossible score, it's that it is not as common for many people to be in this position/condition. However, it might be you - just be completely honest with yourself. No one besides you needs to see your scores.

Having this visual is critical so you can be acutely aware of your current *career transition condition*, address any deficiencies, and understand your life priorities. Once you've made this assessment, you're ready to move on to the most important step… **Identifying Yourself**.

5. STEP TWO: IDENTIFY YOURSELF

In the previous step we discussed, and you discovered, the most important elements of your current condition. Where you are and if you are where you want to be both physically, emotionally, personally, and professionally.

Now, let's talk about what your most favorite things in life are and what your absolute least favorite things are. Don't worry... you won't need to get into too fine detail. Just think about it and begin a list of your top 5 and bottom 5 things you like to do with your time:

COMPLETE SET 1. QUESTIONS:

1. What I like **MOST** to do with my time is _____?

2. What I like **MOST** to do with my time next is _____?

3. What I like **MOST** to do with my time next is _____?

4. What I like **MOST** to do with my time next is _____?

5. What I like **MOST** to do with my time next is _____?

COMPLETE SET 2. QUESTIONS:

1. What I like **LEAST** to do with my time is _____?

2. What I like **LEAST** to do with my time next is _____?

3. What I like **LEAST** to do with my time next is _____?

4. What I like **LEAST** to do with my time next is _____?

5. What I like **LEAST** to do with my time next is _____?

After you've completed this list, think about, and decide, what types of cases you *1.* are best suited/qualified to mediate, and *2.* are most interested in mediating. HELPFUL HINT: "Anything" or "Everything" aren't acceptable answers to these questions. A mediator must be comfortable and confident in their mediation setting, so it is critical for you to complete a very thorough and honest assessment here.

COMPLETE SET 3. QUESTIONS:

1. The cases I'd like to mediate **MOST** are _____?

   Why?: _____

   _____.

2. The cases I'd like to mediate 2nd **MOST** are _____?

   Why?: _____

   _____.

3. The cases I'd like to mediate 3rd **MOST** are _____?

Why?: _____

_____.

4. The cases I'd like to mediate 4th **MOST** are _____?

Why?: _____

_____.

5. The cases I'd like to mediate 5th **MOST** are _____?

Why?: _____

_____.

COMPLETE SET 4. QUESTIONS:

1. The cases I'd like to mediate **LEAST** are _____?

Why?: _____

_____.

2. The cases I'd like to mediate 2nd **LEAST** are _____?

Why?: _____

_____.

3. The cases I'd like to mediate 3rd **LEAST** are _____?

Why?: _____

_____.

4. The cases I'd like to mediate 4th **LEAST** are _____?

Why?: _____

_____.

5. The cases I'd like to mediate 5th **LEAST** are _____?

Why?: _____

_____.

COMPLETE SET 5. QUESTIONS:

1. The cases I'm **BEST** suited to mediate are _____?

   Why?: _____

   _____.

2. The cases I'm 2nd **BEST** suited to mediate are _____?

   Why?: _____

   _____.

3. The cases I'm 3rd **BEST** suited to mediate are _____?

   Why?: _____

   _____.

4. The cases I'm 4th **BEST** suited to mediate are _____?

   Why?: _____

   _____.

5. The cases I'm 5th **BEST** suited to mediate are _____?

   Why?: _____

   _____.

COMPLETE SET 6. QUESTIONS:

1. The cases I'm **LEAST** suited to mediate are _____?

   Why?: _____

   _____.

2. The cases I'm 2nd **<u>LEAST</u>** suited to mediate are _____?___?

   Why?: _____

   _____.

3. The cases I'm 3rd **<u>LEAST</u>** suited to mediate are _____?

   Why?: _____

   _____.

4. The cases I'm 4th **<u>LEAST</u>** suited to mediate are _____?

   Why?: _____

   _____.

5. The cases I'm 5th **<u>LEAST</u>** suited to mediate are _____?

   Why?: _____

   _____.

Now, compare your answers to the Set 3. Questions to your answers to the Set 4. Questions. Examine each question and answer along with the rationale *(Why?)* for your answer. If this examination causes you to reconsider any of your answers, record your new answer and be open to moving an answer from one category to the other (i.e. from what you like **<u>MOST</u>** to what you like **<u>LEAST</u>**).

Next, compare your answers to the Set 5. Questions to your answers to the Set 6. Questions. Examine each question and answer along with the rationale *(why?)* for your answer. If this examination causes you to reconsider any of your answers, record your new answer and be open to moving an answer from one category to the other (i.e. from what you are **<u>BEST</u>** suited for to what you are **<u>LEAST</u>** suited for).

This process should help you arrive objectively at the types of cases you will enjoy mediating and are best suited to mediate. Remember, you're the only person that is going to read your answers, so be completely candid with yourself.

Last, how much of yourself, your time, and your money are you willing and able to give to this new venture? What is your professional budget and what is your household budget? Don't wing it either. Be as scientific as you can about this part of the assessment. Include your spouse or significant other while making these assessments, as well as any business partners/associates you may have that will influence your final decisions regarding a mediation practice. Can you afford to undertake this career change at this time? Do you need to wait and build your savings? Would it be best for you to pursue a mediation career at 50% rather than 100% of your income? Would 25% or 10% be more reasonable, or would that just not be worth the transition demands? Look before you leap. Think before you move. Measure twice, cut once. Be intentional.

6. STEP THREE: IDENTIFY YOUR TARGET

Now that you have a better understanding of current emotional, health, personal and professional status, commitments, wants and needs, it's time to determine *where* you need to go and *who* you need to meet to begin building your mediation practice.

This will be determined in great part based on your answers and revelations in Steps 1 and 2. Where and how each of us spends our time is greatly directed by our thoughts, dreams, aspirations likes and dislikes. So, remember to be completely honest with yourself here. If you really don't *like* playing golf, then don't put it on your "like" list. So, let's identify your *preferred reality* as to how *willing* you are to adapt and change how you spend your time. I promise you have more control over this than you might think.

Next, the *types of cases/problems* you will want to help others settle should be a healthy combination of what you want to do and what you're naturally good at. If you think you're on fire to mediate co-parenting disputes, but you hate being around irrational, self-centered *(defensive, and territorial)* people you will want to reconsider this. It's not that parties disputing over parenting issues are irrational or self-centered, it's that this is the behavior you can expect from many of them at mediation. They're not in the best place in their lives right now, so we shouldn't necessarily expect calm, rational behavior. Likewise, if your strong suit as a mediator has to do with another set of professional skills you possess (construction issues, contracts, personal injury, etc.) that arena/type of case might be the best fit for your practice focus. Ultimately, the final answers to these questions will determine which court and dockets these types of cases will be in/on.

Next, geography matters - a lot. The whereabouts of the parties involved in these cases will generally determine the jurisdiction of their case - and the location of the courthouse – where you will find the cases and the judge(s). Now, just because a case is filed in a particular county doesn't mean that's where all the parties live, nor does it mean that is where the mediation will be held. One benefit mediation *can* offer the parties is ease of access and proximity of the mediation to their locations - when possible. For example, if you are mediating a case in a jurisdiction that is 100 miles from you and the parties and their attorneys are mostly located in that county, it usually makes sense for the mediator (you) to travel to everyone else. Conversely, you might also mediate a case in a jurisdiction 100+ miles from you *(or beyond your usual travel range)* and the parties/attorneys agree to either travel to you, or meet somewhere in between. Either way, you must be aware of this tangent and plan for it accordingly.

Court Clerks in every county can also be extremely helpful in this regard. With one phone call to the Court Clerk you will be able to find out everything you need to know about the case/lawsuit you're going to mediate *(judge's name, courthouse and courtroom location, parking, docket times, Local Rules of Court, etc.).* Building a relationship with the Court Clerk and ALL of their staff will go a long way in building a successful mediation practice. When possible, make your initial meeting in person - names, when combined with faces, change relationships.

Once you have identified the types of cases, docket times, the judge's name and office location, the location of the courthouse, and have started to build a relationship with the Court Clerk and their staff, you will need to find out the schedule of these dockets, or the dates and times these dockets are heard by the judge. Each docket - especially in more rural areas - is on a schedule based on the number of those cases that are filed each month. The types of cases that are filed most frequently will generally be heard by the judge more frequently, and vice versa. For example, if you are in a rural General Sessions court, the judge will have at least five (5) completely different dockets: Criminal, Civil, Pro Se Civil, Probate, and Juvenile. The types of dockets and cases will depend on each judge's jurisdiction. Each of these dockets will hold a variety of types of cases, many of which are eligible for mediation. So, be sure to ask the Court Clerk for a schedule of each docket so you can begin to strategically plan your days and weeks for maximum effect.

COMPLETE THIS:

1. Which counties will I target?: _____

_____.

2. What is the address of the courthouse for each of these counties?: _____

_____.

3. What is the Court Clerk's name and telephone number in each of these counties?: _____

_____.

4. What is the judge's name and telephone number for each of the dockets (types of cases) I plan to target?: _____

_____.

5. What is the schedule for each of these dockets (dates and times)?: _____

_____.

6. Which courtroom is each of these dockets heard in?: _____

_____.

7. Where is the best place to park in relation to the courthouse?

_____

_____.

With this information you'll be ready to begin planning your mediation activities in the next step, **Plan Your Trip**.

7. STEP FOUR: PLAN YOUR TRIP

Now that you know which cases you're going to pursue for mediation, where they are, when they are being heard, and the judge's name, you're ready to plan your day and subsequent days in court and mediation.

First things first. You'll need a checklist to make sure all your bases are covered. Otherwise, you'll probably feel like you didn't accomplish anything when you get home at the end of the day. This is the checklist I use, starting from the time I leave my house, headed to the courthouse:

1. I arrive **in the courtroom** (<u>not</u> ***at*** *the courthouse*) 15-30 minute prior to the docket time (if the docket is at 8:30am, then be there no later than 8:15am). There are a couple of important reasons for this:
   a. I want to get a seat as close to the front of the courtroom and nearest the Bar gate (between the gallery and the Bench) possible;

b. I want to be seated so that they judge has a clear line of sight of me;

c. I want to have an unobstructed view of everyone within the Bar;

2. I introduce myself to the Court Officer(s) or Bailiff(s) immediately – particularly the one that appears to be working closest with the judge. I put a big (professional) smile on my face, introduce myself and explain that I am a mediator and I would like five (5) minutes of the judge's time if and when possible. I treat all court staff like they are the most important person in the world, because they are and will continue to be in this endeavor. Look at it this way, you want to meet the judge, right? Well, they're staff are the most trusted people in the judge's life, so you'll have to get past them to meet the judge. So make new friends with each of them, be yourself and always remember and observe this protocol. Even after you've been in the judge's courtroom several times, still treat their staff with this same respect and dignity. It's the right thing to do, and it will serve you well. I've met hundreds of court staff over the last decade and I can honestly tell you that I have never met anyone that was less than cordial, professional, and helpful. Just extend the same courtesy.

3. While in the courtroom, I **ALWAYS** stand while talking with the judge or if the judge calls my name. Even if it seems that no one else in the courtroom stands when they speak to the judge, be the one that does. Above all else, their position and the Court of Law itself merits that respect. Whether in court or in the judge's chambers (office), the proper salutations for judges are *Your Honor, Judge, Ma'am,* or *Sir.* If you are a non-attorney mediator, this is particularly true as you will be expected to know and observe courtroom decorum.

When I meet with the judge, I keep my word. I said I'd like five (5) minutes of their time, so I make sure I don't go over five (5) minutes unless the judge wants to talk longer. I get down to business immediately - I have my shtick ready and rehearsed. "I'm Clay Phillips and I'm a mediator. I'd like to see if there might be a way I can assist you with this docket by providing same-day mediation services, or scheduling them out within the next 30 days." I wait to see what the judge says, and go from there. This might involve sitting in court for the rest of the docket to see if anyone volunteers for mediation, or the judge might order them as they move through the docket. Oh yeah, while meetings with the judge… most will likely introduce themselves by their first name - or insist that you use their first name. Don't use their first name. Ever. If you have questions refer to #3. above.

8. STEP FIVE: MAP YOUR TRIP

So, now you know *who* you are, *where* you are, *what* kinds of cases you want to mediate, *when* and *where* those cases are located, the Court Clerk's name and telephone number, *who* the Court Officer(s) and Bailiff(s) are, *who* the judge is, *how* early to get to court, *where* to sit, *how* to ask for a meeting with the judge, *how* to address the judge, and *what* to say in your meeting with the judge. You've been to court, you got there early, you've met the Court Officer/Bailiff, you've had your meeting with the judge, the meeting went well, the judge has accepted your offer and you start mediating cases! Woo Hoo! You've made it!

This would be a great time to *hold your horses...* time *to slow your roll.* After the judge accepts your offer, what do you do? How do you do it? What's your plan? How do you deliver on your promises to the judge? Well, you're going to need a very well-planned strategy, process, and system. Your strategy will be the combination of your process and your system. You know how to prepare for mediation, how to mediate, how to conclude a mediation... so there's your process. Now, you just need a system - a system that accomplishes what you promised the judge. Here's the system I created years ago that hasn't disappointed me for more than 10 years:

1. Identify ALL the cases on the docket that are either volunteering to go to mediation or are being ordered by the judge;
2. Schedule all the volunteers' cases to be mediated that day at the courthouse so they can potentially finalize their lawsuit that day - and because they volunteered, I believe they should have first right of refusal to schedule their mediation for another day. If this is their preference, I let them - provided of course the judge has instructed me/them to have it done that day;
3. Schedule all remaining mediation cases to be held at the courthouse and completed within the timeframe specified by the judge *(usually within 30 days of that court date)*;
4. For all of these cases, ask the judge how he/she would like for me to conclude mediation with and without an agreement. "What do I instruct the parties to do once they have completed mediation?" I'll ask the judge this question before court starts.
5. Get any agreement signed, instruct the parties as to next steps - according to the judge's directions, I destroy my notes, and I file my Final Report of Mediator; and
6. I return to court on the next docket date to mediate more cases.

So, what do you do tomorrow? Where are you going? This is when it starts getting really simple – because it's repetitive. Unless you're working in a highly populated or metropolitan area, you will likely have to travel to multiple surrounding counties, find multiple dockets and courtrooms, identify multiple Court Clerks, identify multiple Court Officers and Bailiffs, identify more judges, and introduce yourself all over again, several times. Are you getting excited yet? You should be because this is the formula I created from my years of failures and successes. The formula for successfully starting a mediation practice. This is the formula that still works for me today and it's working for several mediators I've trained and mentored over the years.

When you begin this process, you will find out very soon that most courts at the same level (i.e. General Sessions Court) have the same docket(s) (types of cases) they schedule them in very similar fashions. Usually, the courts' dockets are scheduled on different days of the week and weeks of the month. For example, the General Sessions judge in "County A" will hear all pro se civil cases every other Tuesday at 8:30am, where the General Sessions Judge in "County B" will hear their pro se civil cases on the first Wednesday of every month. Judges schedule routine in their dockets to help expedite the hearings, to help their staff, attorneys, and other court personnel plan other events and cases. Judge's also schedule in this fashion in case they need to fill in for one another *(emergencies, illness, vacation, etc.)*. Once you have established yourself with one judge - and have mediated some cases for them *(over at least three or four court dates)* - it's time to ask the judge about their judge colleagues in the neighboring counties and if they would introduce you to them (usually via telephone or email). In my experience, judges have been pleased to introduce me to their colleagues and several have even given a glowing review of my services and the positive impact mediation has had on their docket(s). So, now you're meeting more judges and now you'll have more court dates to add to your schedule. You'll repeat this until you've met enough judges that want to use your services, and until you are in court three days per week *(reserving the other two days for mediation that has to be scheduled beyond the court date)*.

What also comes with a full calendar is earned credibility and *a place at the table* - or, shall I say, *a place in the courtroom*. Remember, each of these cases will only last (for you) an hour or two, so coming to court as I've described above will be necessary until you begin to secure cases from attorneys. Speaking of attorneys, one of the best benefits of mediating cases on pro se dockets is that you will become a very familiar face in the courtroom in a short amount of time. Not only will the judge and their staff become more familiar with, and fond of you, there will be plenty of attorneys in the courtroom while you're there so it's only a matter of time before you'll meet them and they begin to hire you to mediate certain cases for them. So be sure to take plenty of business cards with you, write your fee schedule on the back of your card, return phone calls within the same day, and build your practice as you go.

As I mentioned, the more frequently you're in the courtroom, the more familiar you will become to others. The more familiar you become to the judge and their staff, the sooner and faster your mediation practice will take root. The more you get appointed to mediate, the more you mediate the more you will become known, and the more you become known the more you will get hired by attorneys.

All you have to do now is repeat Steps 3 and 4 two or three times weekly, for six (6) months you and will see your mediation calendar begin to fill up.

9. STEP SIX: GET MOVING!

So, you're out of the gate and your mediation practice has budded. What's next? It's time to starting living the life of a mediator. The most simple and reliable strategy I can offer you is that if you *aren't* mediating you **have** to be sitting in court somewhere, meeting a judge, talking about mediation, volunteering to mediate or attending a Bar Association luncheon providing a free CLE... or otherwise promoting yourself and your profession. Mediation is an interesting subject and practically everyone I meet is extremely intrigued about mediation and is willing to talk about it. Anyone that knows me knows I'm ready, willing, and excited to talk about mediation anytime, to anyone. So much so, that one of the best compliments I ever got was from a very well-known and respected attorney and mediator in the Nashville area. At a conference one year, he was the host and I was speaking on mediation ethics and he introduced me as "The Evangelist for Mediation". He told the audience I earned this title because I am *always* talking about, demonstrating my passion for, and promoting mediation. Always. I love being a mediator. I love that mediation is a key part of my purpose. I love that I am placed in people's lives during some pretty horrible times and I am able to help them find hope and resolution. I love seeing people leave mediation in a different condition than when they arrived. Because of the empowering effect of mediation, I get to see them in a much better place than when they arrived. Much better than they ever imagined or thought was ever possible. More certain.   More informed.   More empowered.   More hopeful.

Last, but not least... let's talk about fees. What you will charge for your mediation services. Unless you're an established attorney, you will likely need to be competitive *(flexible)* with your fees.

Starting out, a sliding fee scale seemed to work best for me. Even today, I maintain some flexibility in my fee schedule. A sliding fee scale is where your fee ranges *(slides)* based on the parties' ability to pay you with lower and upper ends. If you plan to offer pro bono *(no fee)* mediation services, then your lower-end fee would be $0.00. NOTE: *ability to pay* and *income* are not

the same. Most courts I've served don't just use the parties'
income to determine their eligibility to be declared indigent for
the purpose of paying the mediator's fees (and other related
expenses/fees/costs).   Many states provide a subsidy to
mediator fees for indigent parties. In Tennessee, such funding is
found under Tennessee Supreme Court Rule 38 (TSCR38)
Divorcing Parent Education and Mediation Fund. When a
subsidy such as TSCR38 is used, the judge will determine each
of the party's ability to pay individually. That is to say that, if
one of the parties is declared to be indigent by the judge, they
will likely qualify for the subsidy while the other party does not.
Therefore, the mediator will be compensated *(at the rate prescribed
in the subsidy provisions)* by the parties independent the other. For
example, if your total fee is $200.00 per hour, each party would
expect to be responsible for half of your fee. In the event one
party is unable to pay your fee, then that party's fee portion will
either be waived or reduced. The other party, however, will still
be required to pay half of your fee, unless you also discount or
waive it. To make it quicker and easier for the parties and their
attorneys to understand - and because it is impossible for me to
determine a party's ability to pay - I always base my sliding fee
scale on the parties income. This is an example of what I have
most recently used:

Gross Annual Income *(per party)* **Mediation Fee** *(per party)*

Gross Annual Income *(per party)*	Mediation Fee *(per party)*
Less than $17,000.00	$ 0.00/party/hr, 2-hr max.
$17,000.00 to $21,999.00	$ 25.00/party/hr, 2-hr min.
$22,000.00 to $26,999.00	$ 50.00/party/hr, 2-hr min.
$27,000.00 to $31,999.00	$ 75.00/party/hr, 2-hr min.
$32,000.00 to $36,999.00	$ 87.50/party/hr, 2-hr min.
$37,000.00 to $41,999.00	$ 100.00/party/hr, 2-hr min.
$42,000 and higher	$ 112.50/party/hr, 2-hr min.

In a sliding fee, your upper-end fee needs to be competitive with other local mediators in your skill and experience range. For example, if you are an attorney-mediator I would suggest that your upper-end mediator fee be the same as your full attorney fee. Otherwise, attorney-mediators typically bill the same fee as their attorney fee *(hourly)*. I would recommend that you let the judge determine the parties' ability to pay and remain flexible on your fees. Not everyone can afford a professional mediator but that doesn't mean they should be availed of their services. As a servant of the court, we must do our best to be available for such cases/appointments.

If you are a non-attorney mediator, I recommend that you consider having the upper end of your fee scale about 25% lower than the average attorney-mediator fee in your local area that mediates similar cases and clientele. Another option *(for attorney- and non-attorney mediators)* is to charge a flat fee for a number of hours (generally in 2, 4 and 8 hour blocks) that reflect at least a 10% discount from their hourly rate. This keeps it simple for attorneys hiring you and easier to budget than an hourly rate. For example, if your hourly rate is $200 you might use a flat fee structure like this:

2-hour block = $400
4-hour block = $700
6-hour block = $1,000
8-hour block = $1,300

In this model, the parties (or their attorneys) can better gauge/budget the cost of mediation, which can make you that much more competitive than your colleagues. So, you see that, if the blocks of time were based purely on your hourly fee, a flat fee offers a substantial discount after the first two hours of mediation. For any time over the paid block, I usually charge by the hour based on the hourly average of the fees already paid.

Lastly, I'll share my fee structure rules of engagement with you:

- Be consistent: Set your fees and fee scale and don't change them for at least two years.
- Be reliable: Do what you say you're going to do... do it how you say you're going to do... and do it within the time frame you said you would do it.
- Be confident: Mediation is a process, nothing more and nothing less. Stick with the process and fight every urge you get to complicate it.

Be judicious. Humans aren't capable of neutrality - *including mediators* - because we have consciences, so be committed to being objective and critical.

10. STEP SEVEN: KEEP MOVING!

Building and growing your mediation practice should spiral upward and outward. Always repeating well-received behavior, while scaling your business presence vertically and horizontally.

At the end of each day, be sure to assess your activities. Review what you did, critique what you should do differently tomorrow, commit to these changes, and shut it down *(your work brain)* at the end of the day. Be honest with, and kind to yourself. Don't be too hard on yourself. It's okay to be your biggest critic as long as you're also your biggest cheerleader. Have fun at everything you do... including mediating, and building your mediation practice. Enjoy your life, your spouse, your kids, your family, your pets, your hobbies every day and you will *LOVE* being a mediator.

At the end of each week, re-assess Steps 1. and 2. and adjust where it's necessary. Continue this routine until it becomes second nature and your mediation practice will begin thriving before you know it.

Being a successful, practicing mediator requires all of these things of you, but mainly requires you to be there – you must be present to win. There is no way around it.

Along the way, start living every part of your life as a mediator:

- Be considerate of the problems of others.
- Be kind and just to everyone.
- Be quick to resolve and slow to react.
- Be a master of and take responsibilities for your choices and decisions.
- Harness the power of your decision-making.
- Make better, healthier decisions every day.
- Remind yourself that mediators don't settle cases… we help and teach others to settle their disputes.
- Remind yourself that mediators are responsible for discharging the mediation process and the parties are responsible for the outcome of the mediation.

Final words... Get up and go do it again… every day.

ABOUT THE AUTHOR

Clay Phillips is a mediator, mediator trainer, consultant, and professor of conflict resolution at two universities in his home city of Nashville, Tennessee. During his vast career, he has mediated more than 400 cases spanning a broad array of civil and domestic actions. He has trained more than 1,200 mediators, and is the author of *The Mediator's Guidebook* series on mediator and conflict resolution practitioner professional development. He also created the curriculum for a regionally accredited Master of Arts Degree in Conflict Resolution which, to-date has more than 300 graduates. He holds a PhD in Business Administration *(Organizational Leadership Specialty)*, a Master of Business Administration and a Bachelor of Science in Business Management. He and his wife Deborah – and their fur baby Izzy – live just north of Nashville, Tennessee.

GET CONNECTED WITH CLAY

ClayPhillipsBooks.com
LinkedIn/in/ClayPhillips.com
@DrClayPhillips

www.ingramcontent.com/pod-product-compliance
Lightning Source LLC
Chambersburg PA
CBHW060324220326
41598CB00027B/4414